5-4-3-2-1 Blastoff!
V-2 Rocket, White Sands, New Mexico, 1948

Trailer Travel
Castle Rocks, Sequoia National Park, California, 1959

Phoenix Municipal
Baseball Stadium
Phoenix, Arizona, 1955

Johnston's Frozen Pies
Location unknown, 1955

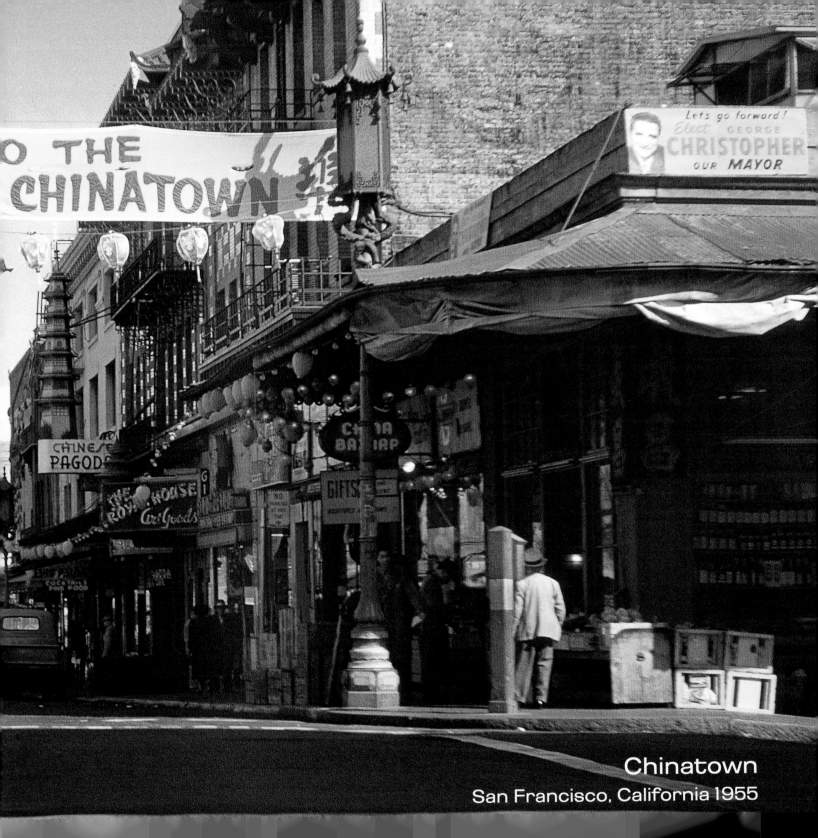

Chinatown
San Francisco, California 1955

Santa's Village
Jefferson, New Hampshire, 1961

Santa's Village
Jefferson, New Hampshire, 1961

Cowell Beach
Santa Cruz, California, 1954

Broadway
Jackson Hole, Wyoming, 1955

Cheesecake
New York Camera Show
New York, New York, 1952

Stardust Casino Resort
Las Vegas Strip, Las Vegas, Nevada, 1958

Aquamaids
Cypress Gardens, Winter Haven, Florida, 1960

AMERICANA
the BEAUTIFUL

Mid-Century Culture in Kodachrome®

Charles Phoenix

Designed by Amy Inouye

ANGEL CITY PRESS

Parading Shriners
San Francisco, California

Americana the Beautiful: Mid-Century Culture in Kodachrome
Copyright © 2006 by Charles Phoenix • www.charlesphoenix.com

Designed by Amy Inouye, Future Studio • www.futurestudio.com

First edition
10 9 8 7 6 5 4 3 2 1
ISBN-13 978-1-883318-54-3 / ISBN-10 1-883318-54-8

Library of Congress Cataloging-in-Publication Data

Phoenix, Charles, 1962-
  Americana the beautiful : mid-century culture in Kodachrome / by Charles
Phoenix ; designed by Amy Inouye.
  p. cm.

ANGEL CITY PRESS
2118 Wilshire Boulevard #880
Santa Monica, California 90403
310.395.9982
www.angelcitypress.com

Summary: 'Here in 144 color pages, with more than 200 color slides, Charles Phoenix tells the story of an era in American history--the Space Age, the Jell-O Salad Days, the Prom Time... yes, indeed, the Mid-Century. A little kitsch here, a lotta love there, some sadness, some joy and most of all, a rollicking good time'--Provided by publisher.

  ISBN-13: 978-1-883318-54-3 (hardcover : alk. paper)
1. United States--Social life and customs--1945-1970--Pictorial works. 2. Popular culture--United States--History--20th century--Pictorial works. 3. United States--History, Local--Pictorial works. 4. United States--Social life and customs--1945-1970. 5. Popular culture--United States--History--20th century. I. Inouye, Amy. II. Title.

EI69.Z8P47 2006
973.92022 2--dc22

                                    2006003473

Printed in Singapore

THANK YOU: Jonathan Behr, Rich Borowy, Cathy Callahan, Paddy Calistro, Bruce Emerton, Jackie Green, D-J Haanraadts, Amy Inouye, Teresa Kennedy, Ed Leibowitz, Lisa Marr, Scott McAuley, Mary Melton, Chuck Morrell, Chris Nichols, Michael Okin, Kieran Sala, Jim Schneeweis.

Images

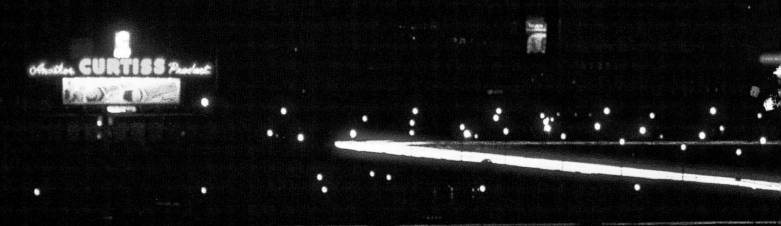

Motorola TV Billboard
Chicago, Illinois, 1961

This neon television clock advertising electronics, home and car radio, and color TV is just east of Lake Shore Drive, near the notorious "S" curve. In the late sixties the iconic sign is demolished to make way for an apartment building.

Storybook Forest
Near Ligonier, Pennsylvania, 1961

Introduction

Obsessively collecting and gleefully sharing orphaned and unwanted family and travel slides from the 1940s, '50s and '60s in books and slide shows is a life force for me. I never dreamed that when I found an old blue shoebox marked "Trip across the United States—1957" in a thrift store in 1992 it would change the course of my life. The box was full of a family's old vacation slides. I held a few slides up to the light and knew instinctively that they were much more than a bunch of so-called "Kodak Moments." I had no idea who these people were, but I knew their slides were a time capsule with my name on it. So I bought them. The vacation these folks had taken nearly a half-century earlier had become a trip back in time and I was now along for the ride. I was so amazed and inspired by this kind of time traveling that I haven't stopped collecting old slides since. The best part is that I get to share the best ones in slide shows that I present to audiences all over the country and in my books.

Searching through old slides looking for great images is the ultimate treasure hunt. It's more entertaining than watching a television show or going to a movie. The sights, scenes and situations are absolutely real, not Hollywood's set-dressed or CGI-wannabe versions of the past. I savor the truth of the images and the beauty of the tales they tell and the places they share. They are fact, not fiction. I love being there for that "Say 'cheese'" moment—wherever 'there' is—even if it's just for that moment, as quick as a click. Slides have taken me to every state in the nation, around the world, inside and out. I've seen children grow up and adults grow old. I've seen the American family in celebration and at work. Slides dispel the stereotypes of the day. They are little picture windows with a view back in time. Each one is a vehicle providing a ride-along to the past.

Fate delivers slides to me in a variety of ways. For nearly a decade I searched for them at thrift shops, estate sales and flea markets. I don't know why people discard them. I never ask. These days they find me more often than I find them. People know I collect, so they bring them to me. Sometimes orphaned slides show up on my doorstep unannounced. I don't know how many slides are in the collection—I stopped counting. I always say it's quality not quantity.

Of course, there are tons of slides that are relatively repetitive and boring. I look past those. The challenge is picking out the best images. If a collection of ten thousand slides yields just one great image interesting enough to share in one of my slide shows or my books, I'm satisfied. Those are the odds I'm playing against. 10,000 to 1. But it's worth it.

The art of being a good collector is being a great editor. I edit each collection as soon as I get it. Otherwise, I'd need a warehouse to store them all. When I look at a slide I look at everything in it, all the details, all the stuff. History is in the details. Really, I'm looking for history more than I'm looking for great photography. I'm also looking for humor and irony. I don't look at the slides; I look *in* the slides. Great images invite you in and make you feel like you're there. I never reject a slide because it is out of focus—if it's a great shot, the mind's eye will put it in focus. This is amateur photography after all. Any images that may be valuable to me or anyone else in the future for purposes historical or otherwise, I keep. Everything else I get rid of. By now I have cataloged countless slides into thousands of subjects and locations, subdivided in hundreds of categories from

Palm Springs to Brasilia, shopping centers to Christmas morning. Keeping track of them all is more than a challenge. The archive takes up half my home. Some slides are identified with handwritten captions; most are not. That leaves me to use clues in the pictures to tell where they were taken. When I find clues, I do further research to find out as much as I can about each slide. I'm always surprised at how much I learn.

The process of creating *Americana the Beautiful* began by choosing the images. I went through tens of thousands of slides before I chose my favorites for this book. I started going through my archive and didn't stop for six months until no slide in the entire collection was left unviewed. Anything unique, unusual or extreme that I thought was a "maybe" was sleeved in categories ranging from "woman in the kitchen" to "Las Vegas" to "taxidermy" to "wallpaper." By process of elimination and by excluding images that I've included in my previous slide-based books, *God Bless Americana: The Retro Vacation Slide Show Tour of the USA* and the companion to this book, *Southern Californialand: Mid-Century Culture in Kodachrome*, I narrowed my choices to a few hundred of the images that would best show off Americana. The two-tone Mercury Turnpike Cruiser spinning on a platform at the 1957 Miami Beach Auto Show, the gentleman's den filled with taxidermy, and Walk-o-Wonders in a suburban

Slide Show
San Jose, California, 1950

"Family Group at Aunt Myrtle's" is written on this slide's mount. Everyone's eyes are fixed on the screen except for the little boy and Grandma, who's dozing off. Grandpa is holding a baby doll.

shopping center parking lot went right to the top of the heap. They are such unusual shots—unlike anything I've ever run across. America's lost theme park, Freedomland USA, was earmarked for several pages. I've never seen any pictures of this short-lived attraction in any book. People posing with their first television sets or their amateur art were set aside. Las Vegas marquees, Florida tourist attractions and anything ultramodern or futuristic began stacking up. These subjects really say Americana to me. Then I began to imagine how the images would best lay out on a page: which would be full-page spreads and which images would unexpectedly complement each other on facing pages. The Oscar Mayer Wienermobile and the Trailblazer monorail are unrelated but look like they were separated at birth, so I put them together. I discovered the flea market scene on Chicago's Maxwell Street, and then I found the slide of three band members posing after the Mummers Parade in Philadelphia. It looks like they are on the same street, but they are not. So close, yet so far away. The lady in the wallpaper shop goes so well with the man standing in the record shop. They make perfect page-mates. The boy's room next to the girl's room is a natural— just like they would be at home.

Throughout the ages man has always found

General Store
Location unknown, 1950s

Fourteen beer-drinking cowboys and one smiling woman pose for a portrait. Cheers! It's a denim fashion show inside a rustic log cabin. The shelves are stocked with Pabst Blue Ribbon and Coors beer, Campbell's Soup, Clabber Girl Baking Powder, Jiffy Pop Popcorn, Van Camp's Pork and Beans, and two stuffed cows.

ways to record his existence and preserve his past. It's a basic human instinct. Cavemen drew pictures on their walls. Americans documenting their America have been no different throughout the years. Photography made documentation much easier as it evolved from its blurry beginnings in the mid-1800s. During the 1930s Kodak colorized photography. The most famous name in film came up with color 35mm transparency film and called it Kodachrome. The modern-day slide show was born. The depth of light and shadow and seemingly infinite palette of rich saturated colors made this new projected medium far more grown-up than any black-and-white Brownie snapshot that came before or after. Decades later, provided that they were stored properly in boxes where it's dark and dry, Kodachrome slides have proven to be fade-resistant, unlike the far less popular other slide film brands of the day. Thanks to Kodachrome, these images of American life look as good now as they did when they were first projected.

Many photojournalists and professional photographers embraced Kodachrome, but most professionals continued to use black-and-white film in their day-to-day work documenting their subjects. Amateur mom- and-pop photographers didn't discover Kodachrome until after World War II when Kodak began marketing the film to a broader market. The timing was perfect. Kodachrome was tailor-made to document the cultural extravaganza the USA experienced during the quarter century from the end of the war to man's unforgettable first

Fun Zone
Los Angeles County Fair
Pomona, California 1962

rocket-ship trip to the moon in 1969. This is the time period this book covers: the space age, the golden age of Americana, the era that most defines American culture. Television, suburbia, shopping centers, the V-8 engine, theme parks, drive-in theaters, Las Vegas and luaus all came of age then too. So did paint-by-numbers, TV dinners, Jell-O molds and rocket ships.

The rocket ship symbolized outer space and outer space symbolized the future. Outer space was not only mass merchandisable, but it became an aesthetic icon. Outer space affected the style and design of countless products—and perhaps nothing was more radically and obviously a symbol of the space age than the tail fins on the family cars of the late 1950s. They represented the future. And in America, "the future" meant optimism. That futuristic attitude captivated the imagination of a generation. Travel and mobility sped up to a dizzying pace. The prop age became the jet age became the space age. Conquering outer space was man's final frontier. The USA had become the world's superpower,

The Tonight Show
New York, New York, 1964

Heeeeeere's Johnny! An NBC Studios studio-audience member snaps this shot of comedienne Kaye Ballard in the spotlight. Her close-up is on the monitor above Johnny, who sits in the dark at his desk on the left. "Color Television" rendered in a fancy red script labels the state-of-the-art camera. First manufactured in 1954, it is the first camera model to capture television in color. *The Tonight Show* made its debut on NBC in 1954, hosted by Steve Allen. Johnny Carson hosts the show from 1962 to 1992.

and being the first country to send a man to the moon was the ultimate proof. Science fiction suddenly became science fact. Progress and productivity unfolded at a pace unlike any modern country had ever experienced. America lived up to its nickname as the "New World." And nothing captured the era more vividly, more realistically, more truthfully than the Kodachrome film that countless moms and pops loaded in their cameras.

All together the vintage slides in this book represent more than a dozen years of collecting. At this point they've come a long way from being someone else's memories to being a part of a collective memory—ours. They teach us a lot about amateur photography, but not nearly as much as they teach us about Americana. There's much more to it than baseball and apple pie. Americana doesn't discriminate between classic and kitsch, high-tech or homespun, mass-produced or one-of-a-kind, the authentic or make-believe. It draws no borders between town and country. It embraces Mother Nature and man-made, the future, the past. Americana is the essence of American culture. These images are *Americana the Beautiful.*

Mullins Grocery Store
Lame Deer, Montana, 1957

Wilson's Meat Chart hangs on the bright yellow wall next to Pierce meatpacker's calendar celebrating happy little piggies, shotguns are for sale and S & H Green Stamps are given away. Green Stamps are given by the checker as a purchase reward at grocery stores and supermarkets across the country. Customers collect and then exchange them for popular merchandise like small appliances or household items at their local Green Stamps store.

Home Sweet Home • Hagerstown, Maryland, 1957

A woman, dressed in a matching coat and hat, totes a rather large cowhide purse. Sharing the porch are two plastic flamingos, an odd little wheelbarrow and the Boston terrier she is tempting with something.

In the basement window sits a stuffed owl and pheasant; in the living room window a stuffed bobcat. Her husband must enjoy hunting. Their Home Sweet Home is actually a house of taxidermy.

The den is a trophy room. A multi-color crocheted granny-square afghan adds some style to an easy chair that matches the curtains. All are set off by wooden checkerboard paneled walls. In case you don't notice the stuffed animals, there are ten reindeer, two foxes sitting on a bearskin rug, one fox hanging from the curtains, a beaver in one window and an owl flying out the other. Have a coat or jacket to hang up? No problem—there are six deer-hoof coat hooks! Need some light? Then turn on the reindeer-hoof lamp. Clearly the male ego works in strange ways. It's one thing to go hunting, but it's another to have stereo vision of your kill when you sit and relax in your easy chair. The dead animals go very well with blond wood and avocado green fabric—it's very earthy.

A Modern Housewife
Tulsa, Oklahoma
1955

Chicken-wire wallpaper, ruffled curtains and a well-dressed woman exactly where society expects her to be—in the kitchen with her modern appliances. She reports for duty in her crisp, clean apron printed with a whimsical carousel motif tied around her cinched waistline with a big bow. She is experiencing a lifestyle of luxury and convenience her mother's generation only dreamed of. With the turn of a knob on her O'Keefe and Merritt stove, she is instantly ready to cook. The stylish washing machine will actually do the laundry for her with a turn of a dial and a push of a button. All she has to do is hang it on the clothesline to dry. If she wishes to witness the miraculous wash-rinse-and-wring event, the machine has a porthole window.

Refrigerator Pride • Danbury, Connecticut, 1953

A woman holding a fatty Porterhouse steak loosely wrapped in plastic is letting all of the cold air out of the refrigerator. Between the big piece of meat, wheel of cheese, two jars of mayonnaise, bottle of mystery sauce, single tomato, bag of carrots, can of apple juice and quart of Borden's homogenized milk, the food pyramid is well represented. The refrigerator is the essential cold counterpart to a hot stove. Together a modern stove and refrigerator address the primal needs of fire and ice and ease the chores

of a homemaker. The refrigerator is the hardest-working appliance in the house. It never stops. General Electric introduced the first refrigerator-freezer combo in 1939. Its job is simple—to preserve food. Other manufacturers introduced refrigerators labeled with explanatory brand names including Coldspot and Frigidaire. The automatic dishwasher is the next major kitchen appliance to bring home-making to a new level of convenience.

Dinner Is Served • Los Angeles, California, 1964

The table is dressed in lace. The silver-plated chafing dish is polished. Serving spoons are in place. This is an artistic and photogenic buffet, and it's time to eat. By the 1960s, molding Jell-O has become an art form. There is an abundance of Jell-O, plain and fancy, sweet and savory. A yellow-and-green striped Jell-O loaf is bordered with radish roses and butter lettuce leaves; an extra large Saturn Jell-O ring sectioned with peas, shredded cabbage and sliced carrots is trimmed generously with ruffled greens. A variety of artificial fruit-flavored Jell-O is served in globs. Edible finishing touches are very important on this table. Cherry tomatoes crown a large pie dish full of potato salad. Green crab apples and pineapple slices frame chunks of fatty ham, while strips of lemon and green pepper top a mound of mystery meat salad. Processed cheese triangles, olives, mushrooms, pickles, cucumbers, deviled eggs, beets and pumpernickel bread complete the appetizing spread.

Meat & Potatoes
Decatur, Georgia 1964

The men of the house experience a moment of family pride posing for a dinner portrait. The life force of the tempting spread inspires a show of primal brute strength from big brother. Together they are about to enjoy sliced Virginia baked ham, roast Tom turkey and dressing, twice-baked potatoes, deviled eggs, green vegetables, baked apples and the centerpiece—a mystery dish. To wash it all down—radioactive poison-green radiator fluid served on ice. And for dessert—matching glow-in-the-dark Jell-O topped with pineapple rings and maraschino cherries.

The Family Couch Portrait • Location unknown, 1957

Two frolicking family members are incognito—one behind a *TV Guide* with Phil Silvers starring as Sergeant Bilko on the cover, and the other disguises herself with a View Master. Sawyer's postcard company in Portland, Oregon, introduced the View Master at the New York World's Fair in 1939. Originally they were sold at stationery stores and scenic attraction gift shops as an alternative to postcards. Each reel has seven 3-D Kodachrome scenic views. They were immediately successful and soon replaced the company's postcard business. On the wall, exotic paint-by-numbers hang on both sides of the figurine-filled blond shadowbox. Paint-by-numbers were also introduced in New York—at the Toy Show in 1951. They were mass marketed by the Palmer Paint Company of Detroit. The instant art kits quickly became a craze that swept the nation. Just three years later, over twelve million had sold. In 2001, an exhibition of paint-by-numbers is displayed at the Smithsonian Institute in Washington, D.C.

The Telephone Call • Nashville, Tennessee, 1960

It's for you! These folks are talking on the phone and reading the deluxe souvenir guide to Knott's Berry Farm and Ghost Town. Opened in 1940 in Buena Park, California, it became America's first permanent theme park. Old Western architecture, attractions, artifacts, displays, demonstrations, costumed employees, souvenirs, food and entertainment are all merchandised together, creating a total immersion environment. Fifteen years later, Walt Disney expanded the concept by creating Disneyland with five different themed realms—Main Street USA, Frontierland, Adventureland, Fantasyland and Tomorrowland. A deluxe Disneyland souvenir guide shares the hassock with two packs of cigarettes, L&M and Pall Mall, and an ashtray full of butts.

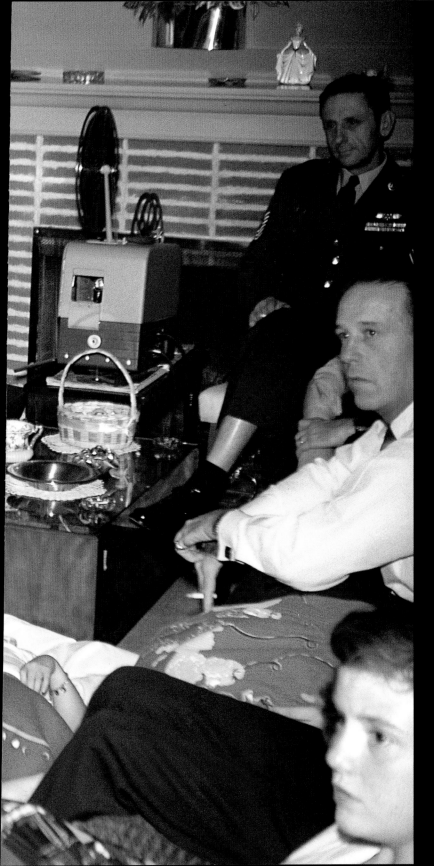

Home Movies
Los Angeles, California, 1957

Tonight this living room with its bright avocado green walls, tropical print curtains and Chinese red couch is a movie theater with wall-to-wall people. Their own reality show is "now playing." The flicker of the film moving through the projector is the soundtrack. The first home movies were taken in 1923 using the revolutionary Cine Kodak 16mm camera. In 1932, during the Depression, Kodak introduced 8mm home-movie film. But it isn't until the 1950s that masses of moms and dads become home-movie makers and movie cameras become a common sight on vacations, at special events and family gatherings. In 1965, Super 8 film is introduced and becomes the last popular home-movie format. By the end of the 1980s home movies are replaced by home videos and movie cameras by camcorders.

A Girl's Room • Location unknown, 1956

Sweet bunny rabbit characters on the wallpaper look like they are straight out of a children's storybook. The alphabet charts are not only decoration; they provide a constant reminder of the bare essentials of education. The bunny and the alphabet are an innocent and simple backdrop for a housewife-in-training proudly displaying her furnished dollhouse. Someone left the tiny toilet seat up. The traditional style of the two-story home is deluxe—just the kind you find in the most civilized neighborhoods in cities and towns across America. The colorful toy home was manufactured by the T. Cohn Tin Toy Company in Brooklyn, New York, and introduced in the 1948 Montgomery Ward Christmas catalog. The price was $4.75; the furniture was extra. Tin dollhouses are closely related to lunchboxes. They are cut and stamped from the same tin and share the same printing process.

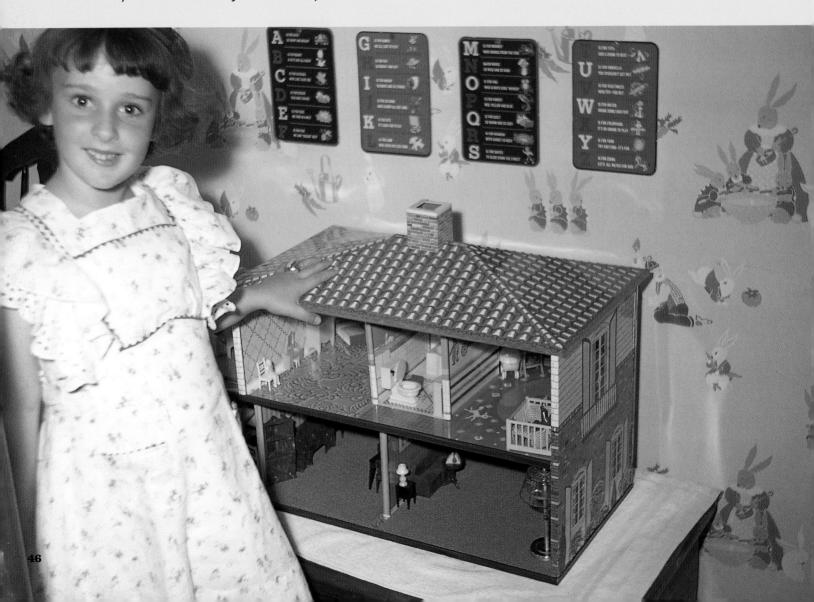

A Boy's Room • Los Angeles, California, 1957

A young man waves the Texas state flag posing at his modern wrought-iron desk. An American flag hangs on the wall. He is allegiant to both state and country. Beside the flag hangs a painting—a primitive snow scene. He's a patron of the arts. A corner radio keeps him informed and entertained. Army barracks-style bunk beds with chenille bedspreads keep him well-rested and warm. On his desk sits a globe and a model of a P-80 Shooting Star jet fighter—just like the ones involved in the massive air raid that never ceases on his wallpaper. He is being psychologically predisposed to participate in warfare. His bedroom is his command center. He is preparing for duty to conquer the world. He practices his aim by shooting darts at the trash can six feet in front him. It's his patriotic duty.

Prom Night
Cleveland, Ohio, 1958

May 17th—formal wear, wrist corsages, high heels, white dinner jacket tuxedos, carnation bouton- nieres and a baby-blue Thunderbird; these slides are marked "Laraine's First Prom." Proms were first held in the 1920s. By the 1940s, they had become the dressiest annual tradition in high schools across the country. Laraine prepares to promenade in her turquoise bedroom. She enhances her tweezed brows with pencil. Pink curlers rolled tight around her short strawberry-blond locks insure the perfect poodle do. In mom and dad's room she gets zipped up while still holding her eyelash curler. The finishing touch of her frilly formal is the tiny blue satin bow set between her breasts with its ribbon streamers falling like twin leashes. In the Early American living room, ready for her date to arrive she strikes a pose before a spinning wheel, ruffled lampshade and candelabra hanging on the terra cotta wall. Beside her a new portable TV with rabbit ear reception piggy backs on the old TV, which has been custom painted avocado green to match the bedroom walls. Outside, a dapper, crew-cut blond shows off a brand new 1958 Thunderbird. Unlike the three previous models—the famous 1955, '56 and '57 two-seaters with their porthole windows and continental kits— the 1958 is the first year of the bigger four passen- ger Thunderbird. Sporty and formal at the same time, the low-slung coupe is picture perfect for these double daters as they drive to the most civilized night of their teenage lives.

Wedding Shower • Somewhere in Florida, 1959

A mop and a broom cleverly disguised as a bride and groom and a laundry basket with a box of Tide. These are among the gifts being given to the bride-to-be to assist her wifely duty of setting up a household and doing her chores. The guests are lined up and riveted. One smokes a cigarette. They all have permanents.

The wedding shower is a traditional ladies-only, pre-nuptial party, the counterpart to the far more raucous bachelor party. Cake and coffee will be served. Hanging on the wall, the garage-made ply-wood crescent moon, with the staircase to heaven, and companion star give the room a mystical quality.

Wedding Party • Somewhere in New Jersey, 1958

The "I do's" have been exchanged. Man and wife pose with their wedding party beside their honeymoon car, a jet-black 1958 Cadillac. The bride's beautiful gown has a scalloped neckline, short sleeves and bouffant skirt. White roses make up her bridal bouquet. The bridesmaids wear emerald green taffeta dresses with cap sleeves, scalloped necklines and tulle veils that easily catch the breeze. They carry yellow chrysanthemums. The groom and his groomsmen sport white dinner jackets over black tuxedo pants accented with tartan plaid cummerbunds and bow ties. White carnation boutonnieres are pinned on their lapels. In the distance you can see a castle turret and the top of Mother Hubbard's shoe, attractions in either a storybook theme park or a miniature golf course.

The Frog Prince

The Old Lady in the Shoe

The Hansel and Gretel restrooms

Dad strikes a pose

STORY BOOK FOREST

Little Miss Muffet

LITTLE MISS MUFFET
SAT ON A TUFFET
EATING OF CURDS AND WHEY.
THERE CAME A GREAT SPIDER,
WHO SAT DOWN BESIDE HER,
AND FRIGHTENED MISS MUFFET AWAY.

Storybook Forest
Near Ligonier, Pennsylvania, 1961

Humpty Dumpty dons a tiny hat on his giant egg head and dresses like Pee-Wee Herman.

HUMPTY DUMPTY STILL ON THE WALL

Smokey the Bear
International Falls, Minnesota, 1958

With shovel in hand and wearing only a ranger's hat and cuffed pants accessorized with a personalized belt buckle, this is the largest statue of the legendary best friend and protector of America's forests. He was dedicated in 1954. In the world of spokes-characters, none are nobler and few are as famous as Smokey. He was created by the National Forest Service in 1944 to keep campers from carelessly destroying the nation's potential lumber supply. His only words are his motto, "Only you can prevent forest fires." Are those two little Smokeys at his side?

Paul Bunyan and Babe the Blue Ox
Bemidji, Minnesota, 1955

Mother and child pose proudly with the superstar of American folklore—the "King of the Lumberjacks." His pet sidekick Babe, the mightiest ox that ever lived, is at his side. Since 1937, the land-of-the-giants scale statues have stood on the shore of Lake Bemidji, where the legendary tale of Paul Bunyan and Babe the Blue Ox is said to have taken place.

Padre Trading Post • Somewhere in Arizona, 1954

Fake cave people are flat-footed and square-shouldered and have outie belly buttons, long hair and bushy eyebrows. Strung artifacts hang around their necks. They wear unisex, fur loincloths. He has fangs, a bone through his nose and baby antlers growing out of his head and threatens with a studded club. And she is topless! These primitive primitives are very inviting. The homemade creatures stand in a vulnerable spot where they very easily could be hit by a car. A uniformed gas station attendant passes by and an early 1950s Cadillac is parked in the background. The Mobil gas station and trading post combo predicts the convenience store concept.

Giant Cement Native American

Near Bryce Canyon, Utah, 1955

A tourist is dwarfed by a rather crude towering caricature measuring in at nearly three stories tall—not counting the feather. The rather startling and unique folk art installation is a magnet to attract eaters and over-nighters to the Canyon Cabins and Café. This grand example of Native Americana is well-dressed for warm weather in his glorified loincloth—two flaps and a waistband decorated with a native bird motif. The look is complete with Indian jewelry, moccasins and headband. He threatens with a tomahawk.

Zozobra • Sante Fe, New Mexico, 1948

A giant marionette gets burned in effigy to dispel the hardships of the past year. Zozobra is the original Burning Man festival. The fiery pageant has been the kickoff of the annual Fiestas de Santa Fe celebration since a local artist created the tradition in 1924. The ceremony includes green and red bonfires, a procession of local men dressed in white sheets called "glooms" and an explosive fireworks display. A band plays a funeral dirge while local men dressed in hooded black robes march before the enormous Zozobra puppet. He flails his arms, rolls his eyes and growls as he meets his fate. The mayor solemnly utters Zozobra's death sentence, then shoots him several times. As he goes up in flames the band plays "La Cucaracha" and dozens of brightly dressed, torch-carrying harlequins dance around him. In 1963 the Kiwanis Club takes over this explosive event and turns it into a fundraiser to provide college scholarships and fund local youth projects and camp fees for physically-challenged children.

Mystery Castle • Phoenix, Arizona, 1958

Like an eerie scene out of an Alfred Hitchcock movie, the golden light of the afternoon sun shines on the sinister monument while a boy stares at the sign. According to the legend, Mystery Castle was built by Boyce Luther Gulley after he was diagnosed with tuberculosis in 1929. He deserted his wife and daughter in Washington and settled on this desolate land just south of Phoenix, where he waited to die. Over the next sixteen years, he passed the time by gathering cast-off building materials to create this folk art house, honoring his daughter's dream of having a sand castle on the beach that wouldn't wash away. After he died in 1945, his wife and daughter learned of his "sand castle" and came to claim it. They liked it so much they moved in. In 1952 Mary Lou Gulley, the daughter, wrote a book called *My Mystery Castle*. She lives beyond the turn of the twenty-first century, continuing to give tours of her unique home.

ENTRANCE
MYSTERY
CASTLE
VISITING HOURS
10AM TO 6 P.M.
DAILY
SUNDAYS AND HOLIDAYS
NO HORSES

Fremont Street • Las Vegas, Nevada, 1958

A '57 Chevy convertible, '55 Buick and '57 Dodge drive through the heart of downtown. A '58 Edsel, with that notorious horse-collar grille, is parked on the left. This is jackpot city. There is no place like Las Vegas. Two short city blocks are packed with a dozen twenty-four-hour gambling halls and saloons. Unlike every other main street in the country, Fremont Street offers jackpots—not goods and services.

The Horseshoe, Pioneer Club, Lucky Strike and Golden Nugget recall the Gold Rush and the Wild West. A giant fiberglass prospector shows off his pan of gold and the neon cowboy Vegas Vic offers Western hospitality and personifies the rustic theme. Fremont Street is the backbone of what becomes the largest city in the USA founded in the twentieth century.

Fremont Street • Las Vegas, Nevada, 1964

Pedestrians are all aglow crossing the most electri-fied main street on the planet. More than the gam-bling, the light show from dusk to dawn makes Las Vegas the most original city in the world. The display is more than impressive—it is empowering. The wink-ing, blinking, flashing, glittering lights are magnetic, intoxicating and liberating. They seduce us. Gambling was legalized in Las Vegas in 1931. With an abundance of cheap electricity after nearby Boulder Dam was completed in 1933, the gambling halls and saloons began to supplement their painted signs and façades with neon to help attract customers at night. With each new electrical addition outdoing the next, the moth-to-a-flame theory was proven over and over again. Unlike New York's Times Square, which adver-tises commercial products on its dozens of electrified animated billboards, Fremont Street sells only the hope of hitting the jackpot.

Silver Slipper • Las Vegas Strip, Las Vegas, Nevada, 1959

A light bulb-studded high heel shoe spins and sparkles day and night, an icon of the Las Vegas Strip. On the left is the entrance to the Last Frontier Village— a mock Wild West town similar to the ghost town at Knott's Berry Farm. On the marquee is Sally Rand, the legendary fan dancer.

The Las Vegas Strip • Las Vegas, Nevada, 1960

There is no better place to pose on The Strip than
with the cement camels and cement Arabs at
the Sahara. They are very photogenic!

Unisphere • New York World's Fair, Queens, New York, 1964

The most spectacular model of earth ever created reflects the lavender glow of twilight. The giant globe is the symbol and centerpiece of the 1964–1965 New York World's Fair. Flushing Meadows in Queens is the site of the fair—the same place the 1939 New York World's Fair took place twenty-five years earlier. Dozens of fountains in a shallow round reflecting pool surround the stainless steel sculpture. When the fair closes in 1965 after its scheduled two-year run, the

Unisphere is among the few World's Fair structures spared the bulldozer. Unlike the Space Needle, the icon of the 1962 Seattle World's Fair that becomes the symbol of the city and a national heritage landmark, the Unisphere is destined to become the most underrated icon of the space age it represents and a lonely reminder of the last great exposition extravaganza held in the USA.

Stardust • Las Vegas Strip, Las Vegas, Nevada, 1959

A big flat Saturn twinkling with multi-colored star-bursts and animated with chasing lights circling the ring sets the standard for neon signs on the Las Vegas Strip. The Stardust opened in 1958. It is the largest casino resort in the world and the first place in Vegas built to accommodate the masses. There are 1,065 motel rooms that rent for six dollars a night.

John Factor, brother of make-up magnate Max Factor, is the owner. The Idiots are performing in the lounge. They share the marquee with the world's largest nightclub revue, the Lido de Paris. The spectacular neon sign remains until 1968, when it is replaced with a far more extravagant, updated version inspired by an atomic cloud.

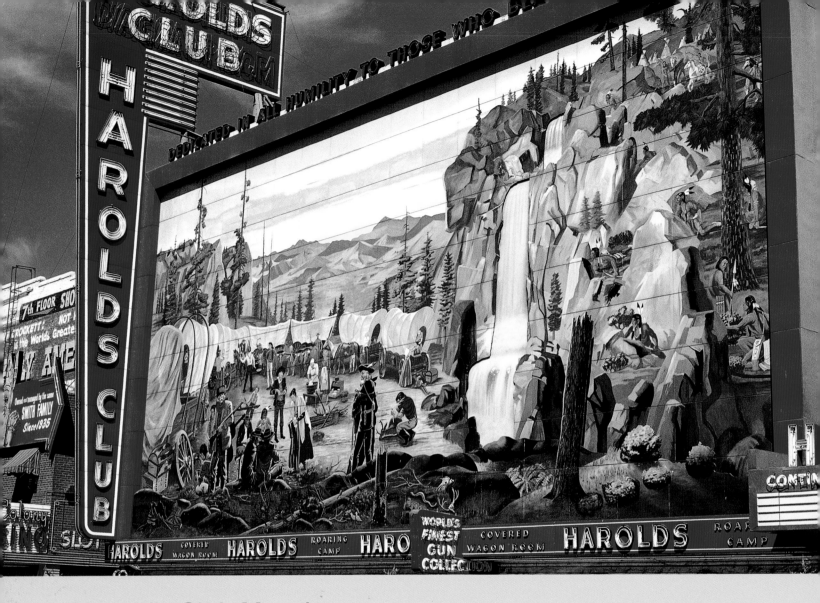

Harold's Club Mural • Reno, Nevada, 1952

Native Americans perched on a rocky mountain cliff observe a pioneer wagon train campsite. After dark the waterfall-to-nowhere lights up and the campfire flickers. "Dedicated in all humility to those who blazed the trails" is spelled out in neon across the top of the lipstick red frame. Neon signage also promotes Harold's Covered Wagon Room, Roaring Camp and World's Finest Gun Collection. The giant-scale Western scene has a distinctive paint-by-number quality. It was commissioned in the late 1940s by Reno gaming pioneer "Pappy" Smith, who established Harold's Club in 1935. For nearly fifty years the work of art is a fixture on Virginia Street. After the casino closes in 1995, it remains in place until shortly before the building is imploded in 1999. Thankfully the mural is preserved and rededicated in June 2005, when it is permanently displayed at the Reno Livestock Events Center.

Primadonna Casino • Reno, Nevada, 1965

Across the street from Harold's Club, an international array of fiberglass showgirls, enshrined like go-go girls, spins seductively beneath glittering orbs. From left to right, eye-catching beauties represent Japan, Spain, USA, France and Africa. The American beauty in the middle rotates on a flattened globe. Perhaps the bright pink, purple, green, hot pink or yellow entice if the showgirls don't. Hungry? Read the breakfast, lunch and dinner menu from the sidewalk.
If none of that is appetizing, then try the Ground Cow

next door. The Primadonna Casino opened in 1955. The giant showgirls went up in the early sixties and stand until the Primadonna closes in 1978. In 1996, the California–Nevada border town of Stateline, between Barstow and Las Vegas, is renamed Primm after the Primadonna owner, Ernie Primm, in recognition of the contribution he made to Nevada gaming—not to mention the fact that the Primadonna Corporation owns all three casinos in his namesake town.

Americana Hotel Lobby
Bal Harbor, Florida, 1957

The hotel guests, modern furniture and flying saucer light fixtures are lost in front of this multi-media room divider—a riot of hypnotic tribal masks, shapes and symbols. It is abstract, mechanical and breathtaking at the same time. "Too much is never enough" is the motto of the hotel's architect and designer Morris Lapidus, who also designed the famous Miami Beach resorts Eden Roc in 1955 and Fontainebleau in 1956. Even the rectangular columns set in a semi-circle and decorated with tone-on-tone tribal patterns compliment the contemporary, everything-but-the-kitchen-sink aesthetic.

Winter Haven, 1954

Ocala, 1964

St. Petersburg, 1964

St. Augustine, 1969

West Palm Beach, 1969

Miami Beach, 1957

Neptune's Gardens • Florida, 1960

Suspended seahorses float in the shadowbox front entrance. A 1957 Mercury bumper provides spectator seating while a woman poses with her two doggies in front of a 1959 Oldsmobile Ninety-Eight. Florida is without a doubt the ultimate vacationland. There is no other state that even comes close to the number of glorified swampland and seashore resorts and roadside attractions.

Luau Party • Waikiki, Hawaii, 1961

An army of tourists experiences the ultimate dinner party of The Islands. Their once-in-a-lifetime dream vacation to Hawaii wouldn't be complete without a luau. The legendary ceremony is a feast of native ambience, food, music and hula dancers, tailor-made for mainlanders who are appropriately decorated with orchid leis and dressed in Hawaiian sport shirts and muumuus. The lady up front in the red-banded muumuu seems to be having a tense moment.

Ti leaves cover the long banquet tables. Tiki torches and candlelit hurricane lamps provide mood lighting. Exotic hibiscus blossoms highlight hollowed-out pineapples and hairdos. Fruity cocktails are served in fresh-cut bamboo tumblers. Roast suckling pig is the main course. Tourists eat "native foods, Island style"—with their fingers. Pounded taro root, a gooey substance called poi, is served in halved coconut shells, and those little white squares are coconut Jell-O. The whole scene is intoxicating.

TRADE WIND
LUAU PA

Trader Vic's • Scottsdale, Arizona, 1966

The obligatory tiki god and tiki torch are the icon and eternal flame of Polynesian pop culture. Together, set in a front yard wannabe-jungle of tropical plants, they mark Trader Vic's entrance. A glorified grass shack, this soaring A-frame structure looks more like a church than a restaurant. The wood shake roof is more suburban ranch house than thatched hut. Trader Vic is the high priest of Polynesian pop. He transformed this desert corner lot into a South

Seas island oasis in 1962. His biggest claim to fame is the Mai Tai, a rum-and-fruit juice cocktail, which he created in his first tropical restaurant bar shortly after it opened in Oakland, California, in the 1930s. Inside and out, his chain of restaurants are total-immersion Polynesian-themed environments, as theatrical as Hollywood movie sets. By the time this location closes in 1990, his namesake restaurants span the globe.

Sambo's Coffee Shop • Lake Tahoe, Nevada 1967

Three customers bask in the glory of orange, yellow, blue and white vinyl, wood paneling, hanging lamps, plate glass and amazing above-the-counter art depicting the coffee shop's namesake, Little Black Sambo. The legendary tale tells the odd story of a turban-wearing Indian boy named Sambo who loses his clothes to some browbeating tigers. They wind up chasing each other around until the tigers melt into hotcakes and butter, which Sambo then eats.

Sambo's began in 1957 in Santa Barbara, California. The owners, Sam Battistone and Newell Bohnett, morphed their names to match the title character in the book by Helen Bannerman that inspired the boy-tiger-pancake theme. Less than a decade later there are 1,200 Sambo's coast to coast and Sam and Bo have a coffee shop empire. By the late 1980s the empire falls, and only the original in Santa Barbara remains in business.

Elias Brothers Big Boy • Bridgeport, Michigan, 1966

Brothers wearing matching Hawaiian shirts pose with Big Boy, one of the most famous hamburger spokes-characters. Like the Statue of Liberty holds her torch, the doe-eyed Big Boy holds a giant version of a double-decker hamburger—his namesake Big Boy—with pride. His big flip hairdo is more like a tidal wave than a pompadour. His brows are high and arched. His trademark red-and-white checked overalls are a major circus clown fashion statement. Everybody knows who he is. He even stars in a comic book series. Bob's Big Boy began as a hamburger stand in Glendale, California, in 1934. Depending where the Big Boy restaurant was later franchised, his name changed—he became Frich's Big Boy in Ohio and Shoney's Big Boy in Kentucky. But the fiberglass clone always stays the same.

Li'l Abner's Restaurant
Seattle, Washington
1962

Hand-painted portraits of characters from Al Capp's *Li'l Abner* comic strip hang in mismatched frames. They are a stark contrast to the monotone avocado green walls and vinyl booths. This is a cross between a pop art gallery and a coffee shop or a museum and a restaurant. Multi-colored plastic fixtures provide lighting for the inspired décor. Li'l Abner is the title character of a popular syndicated comic strip that has run in newspapers across America since 1934 and continues until 1977. He is a hunky, naive man-child who earns his living as a mattress tester. He constantly refuses the advances of his girlfriend Daisy Mae, who is running after him on the wall. Their images flank Schmoo, the oddest-shaped comic strip character ever.

Sidewalk Art Show

Greenwich Village
New York City,
New York, 1958

A Norman Rockwell painting comes
to life. Classic Old World land-
scapes, seascapes and country
scenes are for sale on the street,
bound for conservative living
rooms. Among the admirers are a
redhead, two men wearing hats
and a picture-perfect little girl.
She is more than proper in her
matching white dress, ribbon-
trimmed hat and Mary Janes worn
with anklets. The front end of an
emerald green 1954 Chevrolet and
the tail of a lipstick-red 1956
Oldsmobile parked at the curb
frame her very nicely.

Amateur Art • Pittsburgh, Pennsylvania, 1960

Pearl Rogal stacks her paintings on the floor, piano bench, desk and fireplace mantel of her Pittsburgh home. Some are framed and some are unframed. She is a frustrated actress who earns her living teaching poise and confidence. On the opposite page, other creative types display their pursuit of artistic excellence. The man on location painting Monument Valley in Utah renders the landscape in warm tones— that's his artistic license. The lady with three birds flying on her wall shows her bird portrait and

mountain lion scene. Blondie, with curls of spun sugar, poses with a self-portrait next to a French Provincial chest of drawers. The classic Old World countryside print on the wall doesn't quite have the heart and soul of the primitive landscape held by the somber artist. The colorful ceramic tile mosaic of a dodo bird driving a train with a giraffe on board is somewhat abstract and entirely kooky. Chances are that these inspired works are all destined for thrift shops.

Ceramics Class • Somewhere in Massachusetts, 1957

According to the institutional-style clock, it's 9:00. Ceramics class is in session. The teacher and his pupils are beaming with joy as they explore the endless possibilities of their individual creativity. They are working in the earthiest of all artistic media—clay. These ladies of leisure exercise their artistic prowess and try their hands at the ancient art of pottery. Each of the ladies wears bright red lipstick and an Easter egg-colored sweater. Among the works in progress are the most elementary of vessels. The gleeful lady in avocado green is the most advanced. She is sculpting a lamb.

Braiding Rugs • Hagerstown, Maryland, 1953

Strips of wool cut from worn-out winter clothes and old blankets are handcrafted into decorative and durable floor coverings—it's a rug-braiding bee. These ladies carry on the Old World and Early American skill of rug making. It's a tradition that has been handed down for generations. Their creative color combinations complement the plaid curtains, red sofa and honey-blond wood floors and furniture in this contemporary living room.

Alpine Concrete Products • Northern, California, 1959

The artist's palette and paintbrushes suggest the artistic quality of the cement animals, religious figurines, lawn jockeys, bird baths and fountains. This is garden art and yard décor. The figurines are very heavy and solid as a rock. If Mother Nature doesn't populate your yard with threatening grizzly bears, reindeer, ducks, swans, foxes, dogs, frogs, roosters and squirrels, you can do it yourself. The concrete clones seem to have stepped out of a giant paint-by-number painting. They are molded by the dozen in a factory and then airbrushed by artists for that authentic look. If fauna isn't what your yard needs, perhaps you're seeking some sculpted spiritual guidance. If so, choose between the faiths of East and West—Buddha and St. Francis.

Bar-B-Q Ranch Western Wear • Post Falls, Washington, 1964

It's the middle of the day and the neon sign is on. A mock black horse is the cherry-on-top of this country-western supply superstore. He is towering above a colt, mare, elk, lion, bear, rooster, purple dinosaur, milk cow, two steers and a cowboy on a bucking bronco displayed on the rooftop. They are all impostors. The fiberglass figurines are manufactured to be used for commercial purposes. They attract customers to roadside attractions and other businesses—cows for dairies, big roosters for fried chicken stands and steers for steakhouses. On each side of the front door a hand-carved wooden Indian greets guests. A 1960 Ford Country Squire, a Rambler American and a horse trailer park in the dirt lot. Women and children mannequins model Western clothes behind the plateglass display windows alongside fiberglass deer. In the A-frame window, a tall cardboard cowboy cutout promotes America's most famous fashions, Levi's.

S.S. Grand View Ship Hotel • Bedford County, Pennsylvania, 1957

Permanently docked miles away from the nearest ocean, the most famous landmark on the Lincoln Highway is a fake. At first glance the *S.S. Grand View* almost looks real. There's even a lighthouse. It began in the 1920s as a mock castle. In 1932 it was remodeled to look like a great steamer and the name was changed. Nautical paintings decorate the dining room. Waiters dress in naval uniforms. The manager is "the captain." A ship's wheel, life preservers and telescopes add to the effect. Business was bustling until the Pennsylvania Turnpike opened in 1940. The dilapidated hotel is sold in 1978 to new owners who rename it Noah's Ark. After a few months the aging ship closes again and falls into even further disrepair. "Save Our Ship" efforts are organized by local preservationists. After years of hard work their dreams of re-opening the hotel go up in smoke. On October 26, 2001, the old ship mysteriously burns to the ground.

Harold's Gas Station • Spring Hill, Florida, 1965

It has just rained. Bright pennants rustle in the breeze. Fluorescent lights are spread like the wings of a pterodactyl. The gas station was built in 1964 in honor of the Sinclair Oil Company's mascot, the dinosaur. Miniatures top three of the four pumps. The primeval architecture looks like a life-size brontosaurus that has been skinned, draped over a form and covered with stucco. The service bays are between the legs, in the belly of the beast. A 1964 Pontiac pulls away from the pump. A 1958 Chevrolet station wagon sits in front of the Coke machine and the men's restroom. When the Sinclair Oil Company stops selling gas in Florida in 1968, the dinosaur becomes an auto repair shop. The roadside novelty endures as the town's most unique attraction for many years.

Holiday Sands Motel • Virginia Beach, Virginia, 1957

If the legendary modernist Piet Mondrian ever painted a motel, this would be it. The Dutch artist is famous for his bold, primary-color-block paintings and this could be one of them. The intoxicating combo of lemon yellow, lipstick red and cobalt blue unexpectedly paired with sea foam green and titty pink is more than eye-catching. It is truly inspired. Coincidentally, the jet-black 1952 Buick, forest-green 1956 Chevy and red-and-white 1955 Pontiac parked out front are color-coordinated. No focus group was asked to come up with the hard-to-miss color scheme, nor asked to comment on it—this is a mom-and-pop motel. Bright colors sell motel rooms.

Mickey Mantle's Holiday Inn
Joplin, Missouri
1962

According to legend, baseball's Hall-of-Famer came up with the hotel's fried-chicken restaurant slogan, "In order to get a better piece of chicken you'd have to be a rooster!" Besides Elvis, the Holiday Inn is the most famous name to ever come out of Memphis, Tennessee. The motel chain destined to become worldwide began there in 1952. The 1942 movie *Holiday Inn* inspired the name. The Holiday Inn signs are perhaps the most memorable and instantly recognizable roadside clones ever created. Sprouting from a flagstone planter the iconic, eye-catching orange, yellow and forest green signs stand out from everything around them. The optimistic pseudo-handwritten font is backhand. The super starburst on top is like the tip of a magic wand. By the late 1980s the iconic Holiday Inn signs are all bulldozed. Not one remains standing.

Sears • Honolulu, Hawaii, 1954

Smart modern architecture two-toned in the decade's signature colors: sea foam green and titty pink. Deep-dish display windows run the length of the store. The corner showcase is dressed in a Japanese theme with a pagoda, teahouse, hanging lanterns and cherry blossoms. The American flag is the crowning touch. In 1959, twenty years after this store opened, Sears leaves this location and moves to a much larger store at the new Ala Moana Shopping Center, nearby in Waikiki. This store becomes the headquarters for the Honolulu Police Department. In the 1990s the building is demolished to make way for an apartment building. Sears is an American institution—the ultimate modern-day general store. The granddaddy of all retailers has convenient catalog stores and sprawling department stores across America. The first store opened in Chicago in 1925, thirty-nine years after Sears began as a mail-order business selling jewelry and watches in 1886.

Kuhio Theater
Honolulu, Hawaii
1946

Circles on circles, squares on squares, curves on curves and stripes on stripes. This is an architectural sampler platter. The style is Streamline Moderne with a heavy-handed Victorian sensibility—a stark contrast to the utilitarian style of the delicatessen across the street. The fashionable movie theater was completed in 1941. But just before the grand opening, Pearl Harbor was bombed and the big grand opening party was postponed until after World War II. During the war, the army took over the theater and used it for storage. Finally the theater opened for business in the summer of 1945. After decades as a single-screen cinema, in the 1980s the 880-seat house is divided in half and becomes a twin-plex. It is demolished in 1996 to make way for a shopping center.

Dari-Delite • Location unknown, 1959

The soaring roofline provides shade by day and light by night. The giant penguin mascot and ice-cream-cone cutout sitting on the roof are big enough to see a block away through the windshield of a car—like the turquoise-and-white 1958 Plymouth Savoy parked out front. Inside are shiny stainless steel soft-serve machines and a uniformed employee serving the customers waiting in line. Cartons of cigarettes are stacked in the lower left corner. Paper cutouts taped inside the plate glass window celebrate Hawaii, our fiftieth state, by promoting pineapple toppings. Everything about this soft-serve ice cream stand is as unpretentious and inviting as the Dari-Delite font. Size-wise the building is tiny but has a big spirit—it epitomizes the no-nonsense form-follows-function fast-food stand style of the fifties.

Jefferson Drive-in Theater • Dallas, Texas, 1953

Now Playing—*Invaders from Mars* and *Laura*; a double bill with a monster movie and a romance thriller. The show starts at dusk. Both films are destined to become classics. The marquee is pure eye candy with neon circles, stripes and squiggles frantically animated before, during and after showtime. A 1949 Chevrolet fits right in with its tropical color scheme of aquamarine and purply pink. The screen tower is like a backyard swimming pool, only vertical. A calypso dancer motif repeats inside the giant floating amoeba. The Jefferson Drive-In opened in 1949 and continues long past the heyday of drive-ins. The final screening is in 1990. The theater closes but remains standing until 2004, when it is torn down to make way for a school.

The Walk-o-Wonders, Great Western Shopper's Mart
Columbus, Ohio, 1958

The Sphinx and Pyramids, Eiffel Tower, Parthenon,
Niagara Falls, Taj Mahal, Grand Canyon, Leaning Tower of
Pisa and Carlsbad Caverns are the "Seven Wonders" of
the parking lot. They are all built to scale in miniature on a
700-by-60-foot rectangular island in front of a suburban
shopping center.

The Walk-o-Wonders, Great Western Shopper's Mart
Columbus, Ohio, 1958

The Parthenon and Albers Super Market's clock tower sign board are an unexpected duo—architecturally and otherwise. Just beyond the plaque on the right is a square viewing hole. Inside are the Carlsbad Caverns. The developer came up with the parking lot gimmick not to lure customers, but to sway potential merchants away from other proposed shopping centers. Creating the worldly wonders was no small task. They took nearly two years to complete.

The amazing display is promoted as the "Nine Wonders of the Modern World" and dedicated to schoolchildren and adults for their enjoyment and education. Between buying poultry, picking up the dry cleaning or trying on a pair of shoes at Thom McAn, shoppers may be able to learn something. In the late 1960s, after years of exposure to the elements and the need for parking spaces, the wonders are demolished one by one. In 1972, the Eiffel Tower, the last wonder standing, is removed and replaced by a Fotomat booth.

The Parthenon

Taj Mahal

Grand Canyon

Leaning Tower
of Pisa

Main Street
Houston, Texas
1956

A blind accordionist sere-
nades passers-by. A seeing-
eye dog stands by his side.
Uncle Tom's Peanut truck
turns the corner. Two ladies
about town are headed inside
the Lamar Hotel. The horn-
rimmed glasses neon sign
above them is also seen on
the left between the Lamar
Hotel and the Metropolitan
Theater where *Hot Blood*
is playing in Technicolor
Cinemascope. Colorful two-
tone cars and buses head
uptown and downtown.
This is the backbone and the
central nervous system of
the city, an evolution of
where the town began just a
few generations before.
Like downtowns in major
cities throughout the country, Main Street in Houston
is threatened by the development of new suburban shopping centers. Over the next
few decades the very founda-
tion of vitality and commerce
in the city erodes. Forty-
seven years after its grand
opening in 1926, the Metropolitan is demolished in 1973.
The Lamar Hotel is razed in
1985.

Lingerie Shop • New Orleans, Louisiana, 1954

The neon sign from the Prevue Lounge across the street reflects in the plate glass window. Inside the window, a single mannequin modeling a silk chiffon peignoir set is non-threateningly seated with her legs crossed and holding out her palms. She poses in a provocative display with a supporting cast of torsos and busts showing the latest in unmentionables. Pink satin bows on the hipbone, belly button and cleavage trim a sheer lace set up front. Across the back is a trio of bathing suits—lipstick red with close-set straps, a black-and-white penguin tuxedo and a racy two-piece in zebra stripes. Garter belts and brassieres fill in the empty floor space. Fake roses, daisies and violets from the millinery supply shop add color. A layaway plan is promoted on cobalt blue Lucite.

Marshall Field's • Chicago, Illinois, 1959

A woman strikes a dramatic pose with a banana. The banana is as real as she is. The plastic tropical fruit is the unexpected focal point of this window display. The mannequin is designed to be holding a mirror. The other two mannequins look away. The giant Barbie-like dolls are dressed in the latest paisley scarf-print styles for resort wear. Each of the beauties possesses the regal and proper poise of a big-city sophisticate. Palm fronds and wicker monkeys holding littler wicker monkeys complete the mood. Marshall Field's has a reputation for having the most spectacular windows in town. The fine department store began in Chicago in 1852.

Wallpaper Shop • Stanton, Missouri, 1962

A wall of wallpaper samples—a buffet of patterns to choose from. The wallpaper saleslady stands guard. Before her on the table are more samples bound in enormous swatch books. Wallpaper is like gift wrapping. Instead of wrapping the outside of the box it wraps the inside of a room. Far more delicate and refined than any wood, stone, brick or paint, wallpaper makes a fashion statement while dressing up a room and giving it a theme. It's a luxury, not a necessity, and simply makes a room special. Wallpaper was once a privilege only for the rich but is now mass-produced to suit every budget. There are countless choices from dozens of manufacturers. Motifs range from bold and bright to meek and mild. An endless selection of styles is sampled; there are conversational, classic, traditional and modern patterns. Most are available in several color treatments. Some are flocked, some are foiled. Florals are perennial favorites.

Jazz Record Store • New Orleans, Louisiana, 1957

Plastic-wrapped jazz 33⅓ rpm records are displayed for sale. Titles include *Johnny Wiggs*, *Jam Session on Bourbon Street*, *The Dukes of Dixieland*, *Dixieland Mardi Gras* and *Burke*. The shopkeeper, posing behind a red bongo drum, predicts the Pee-Wee Herman look—a gray glen-plaid suit, white shirt and red bow tie. Busts of classical composers and a philodendron in a red foil-wrapped pot share the eye-level shelf with tambourines, maracas, a tin drum and a metronome. A painting of a Dixieland band hangs on the wall.

Oscar Mayer Wienermobile • Upstate New York, 1964

Little Oscar greets parade-goers from the open cockpit high atop the world's most famous product-shaped promotional vehicle. He is dressed for duty in his chef's uniform. At the end of the parade the Oscar Mayer ambassador will give away wiener whistles to the kids, sign autographs and pass out free samples of Oscar Mayer products. Oscar Mayer began selling wurst in a small Chicago meat market in 1883. His first hot dog-shaped vehicle was built in

1936. Several generations of Wienermobiles followed. Between 1950 and 1954, five new Wienermobiles were built. This is one of them. The big weenie with wrap-around tinted glass windows sits on a flattened 1950 Dodge. In 1991, one of these second-generation Wienermobiles is removed from storage, restored and displayed at the Henry Ford Museum in Greenfield, Michigan.

Trailblazer Monorail • Texas State Fair, Dallas, Texas, 1960

This high-tech hot dog in the sky would be the Wienermonorail, if it was sponsored by Oscar Mayer. But it isn't. Originally called the Skyway, it was built in 1956 at Arrowhead Park in Houston, Texas as a prototype transportation system. Developers claimed the space-age vehicle would be the future of mass transit and the quickest and cheapest way to solve the city's traffic problems. The sleek fiberglass-bodied coach has wraparound Plexiglas windows and seats sixty passengers. Two Packard V-8 automobile engines provide the power. It never reached the projected top speed of 80 mph on the short 900-foot test track. Thousands received free test rides during the eight months it ran. After Houston city officials rejected the progressive idea, the monorail was dismantled and sold to the Texas State Fair in Dallas, where it was reconstructed and rechristened the Trailblazer. It remains there until 1963 when it is demolished and scrapped.

Maxwell Street Market • Chicago, Illinois, 1957

A woman stares daggers through a dozing peddler. He dons the unexpected combination of a Shriner's fez, sunglasses and a full head of long bleached-blond hair. Maxwell Street is located about a mile southwest of Chicago's "magnificent mile." It's the town's tender underbelly, a rare place where Jews, blacks, whites, Asians and Latinos feel comfortable mixing. They wheel and deal for bargains, play cards, eat ethnic food and listen to street musicians play live jazz. Urban critics claim the area is among the worst slums in the country. Others describe it as the soul of the city or the Ellis Island of the Midwest, drawing migrants from distant parts of America and immigrants from all over the world in search of a better life. By the early 1990s, nearly a century after it began, gentrification and urban development all but erases this alternative marketplace.

Mummers Parade • Philadelphia, Pennsylvania, 1955

It's New Year's Day and this musical trio has just marched in a band with dozens of others in the parade. Their uniforms are spectacular in shocking pink and royal blue satin. Like all the other bandmates, they look like toy soldiers with those bright circles of rouge on their cheeks. It's cold, so they wear gloves with cut fingertips so they can play their instruments. Thousands of locals celebrate each New Year's Day by marching in the Mummers Parade wearing colorful costumes generously trimmed with beads, sequins and feathers. The tradition began in the 1700s when Swedes, who settled just outside of Philadelphia, rang in the New Year by parading in the streets and creating a ruckus by ringing bells and firing gunshots. Over the years the partygoers gave up the guns for other noisemakers and the costumes became more elaborate. In 1976 a museum dedicated to the Mummers Parade opens in Philadelphia.

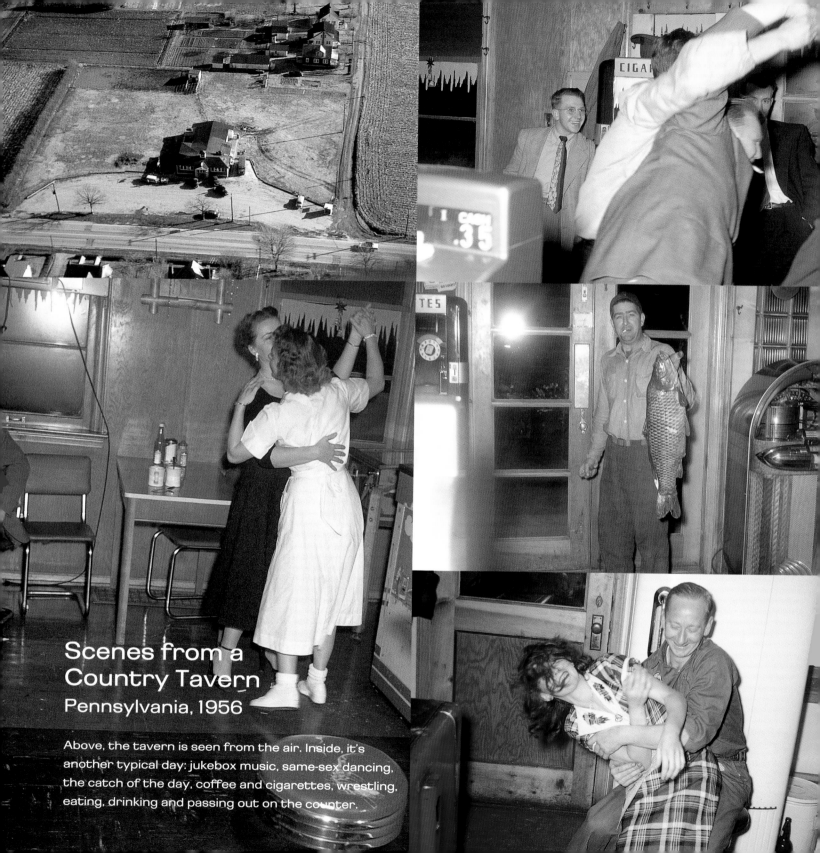

Scenes from a Country Tavern
Pennsylvania, 1956

Above, the tavern is seen from the air. Inside, it's another typical day: jukebox music, same-sex dancing, the catch of the day, coffee and cigarettes, wrestling, eating, drinking and passing out on the counter.

Camel Billboard • Times Square, New York, New York, 1964

A puff of steam that looks like cigarette smoke blows from a giant portrait of New York Yankee outfielder Roger Maris. The baseball legend, best known for hitting sixty-one home runs in 1961 is the current famous face exhaling Camel smoke every four seconds. The billboard went up on the Hotel Claridge at the southeast corner of Broadway and West 44th Street in 1941, during World War II when lights in advertising were banned. A clever ad man came up with idea of having the Camel Man blow smoke across Broadway to attract attention to the unlit billboard. The puffing continues night and day until 1966, when the hotel is demolished and the billboard puffs its last puff.

Planters Peanuts Billboard
Times Square • New York, New York, 1958

Mr. Peanut waves his walking stick between the giant cocktail can and enormous snack-sized bag of the salty treat he represents. Otherwise he is fixed in a feminine pose. A wall of 15,000 glittering lights ensures that he doesn't go unnoticed after dark. Red neon flashing "Planters Peanuts" matches the red lips that frame his toothy grin. Mr. Peanut has style and class. He wears a monocle over his left eye and sports accessories associated with formal attire—but no clothes. His shell is his suit. Mr. Peanut was born in 1916, the brainchild of a fourteen-year-old boy who cleverly morphed nut and man and created one of the most enduring and dapper trademarks ever. The billboard went up on Broadway between 46th and 47th streets in 1942. Originally it was over the store that occupied the retail space below. When the store closed, the billboard stayed. Planters Peanuts began in 1906 in Wilkes-Barre, Pennsylvania.

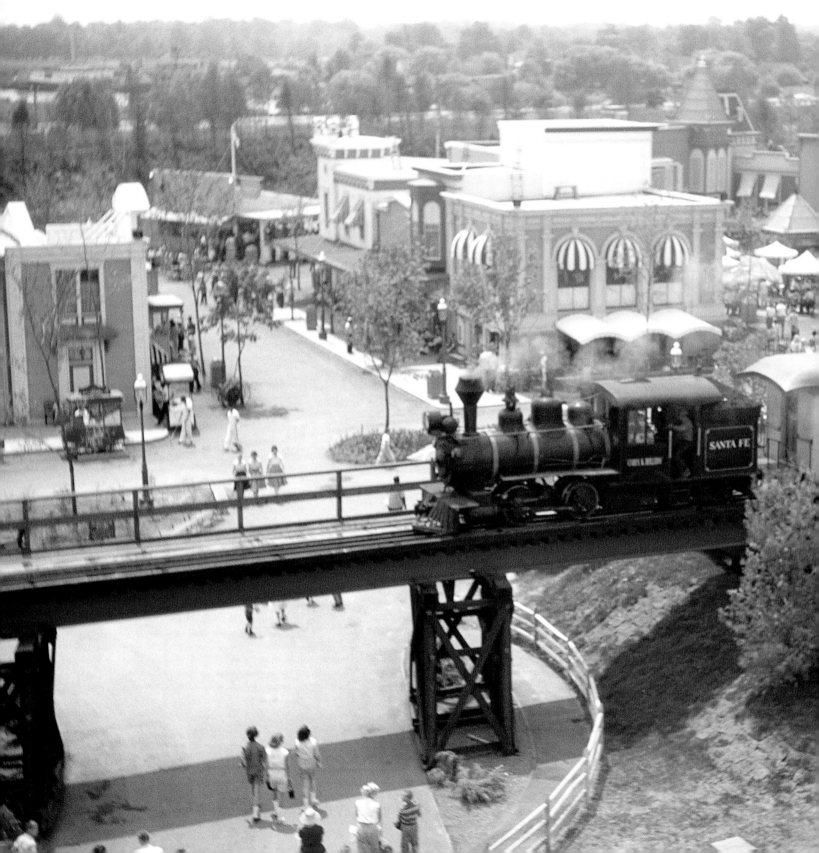

Freedomland USA
Bronx, New York, 1961

Freedomland USA is America's lost theme park. The Santa Fe train chugs away from the station in the town square. The charming turn-of-the-century scene bears a striking resemblance to Main Street USA at Disneyland. The short-lived attraction is an exciting panorama of American history laid out in the shape of the United States. Seven "lands" each represent a different part of the country—the Southwest, old New York City, New Orleans at Mardi Gras, San Francisco in 1906, the Great Plains, Chicago in 1871 and the satellite city of the future. Located just thirty minutes from the heart of New York City in the Bronx, it's the world's largest theme park—more than three times the size of Disneyland and nearly four times more expensive to build. On the evening of opening day, June 19, 1960, Ed Sullivan introduced Freedomland USA to his television audience as Disneyland's equal on the East Coast. C.W. Wood, one of Walt Disney's primary movers and shakers during the planning, construction and opening of the Magic Kingdom, came up with the idea. He convinced one of the East Coast's most powerful industrialists to finance the park. Doomed from the start, Freedomland USA files for bankruptcy and closes just four years after it opens. Park officials claim the competition from the 1964 New York World's Fair is the straw that broke the camel's back. In the late 1960s, the single largest residential development in the United States, thirty-five high-rise apartment buildings called Co-op City, is built on the site.

Main entrance

Fort Calvary

Old Chicago train station

Fort Calvary

SS Americana

Sky Buckets

Freedomland USA • Bronx, New York, 1960

Above, in Old Chicago, visitors help battle the fire of 1871. The legendary event occurs every twenty minutes. Then there's a fire sale in the curio shop. But that's not all of the doomsdays in the mix. In New Orleans a tornado ride takes you inside the eye of a powerful twister. In San Francisco the earthquake of 1906 happens over and over again inside a dark ride. Holdups, bank robberies and gunfights happen regularly in the Old West. A stagecoach ride takes guests over the Lewis and Clark route and through Civil War battlefields. Not all of the attractions are so tragic. The *S.S. America* travels around a twenty-million-gallon replica of the Great Lakes. The sky buckets go to the top of the Rocky Mountains. A working farm sponsored by Borden has Elsie the Cow, a barnyard full of animals and a cornfield.

Satellite City • Freedomland USA, Bronx, New York, 1960

Visitors board the Braniff Airlines-sponsored Space
Rover Flying Saucer for a thrilling six-minute trip into
orbit. They will see a panoramic view of the western
hemisphere.

Space Needle,
Seattle World's Fair
Seattle, Washington, 1962

The spectacular restaurant-cocktail lounge-observation deck combo is the symbol and center-piece of the futuristic century-21-themed 1962 Seattle World's Fair. According to legend, the original design for the orange UFO perched high atop a tripod landing pad was drawn on a cocktail napkin in a bar. It is destined to be the world's greatest architectural icon of the space age. In 1992 it is declared a cultural heritage landmark.

Landmark Hotel Casino
Las Vegas, Nevada, 1972

Designed in the late 1950s, this is by far the most futuristic hotel ever built. It bears a striking resemblance to the outer space architecture seen in *The Jetsons* cartoon, which debuted in 1963, the same year construction of the thirty-one-story, five-hundred-room, flying saucer-style hotel/casino was completed. But for mysterious reasons it didn't open for business until 1969. Never very successful, it closes in 1990 after years of decline. On Tuesday, November 7, 1995, at 5:35 A.M. the Landmark is imploded to make room for a parking lot.

Oral Roberts Prayer Tower
Tulsa, Oklahoma, 1969

This skewered spaceship is the Oral Roberts University visitors' center. The heavenly two-hundred-foot creation was built in 1967. An eternal flame burns high atop the tower. The observation deck houses the Abundant Life Prayer Group, where dedicated men and women pray with people by telephone twenty-four hours a day.

Busch Gardens • Tampa, Florida, 1960

Lutheran Church • Los Angeles, California, 1965

Travelers Insurance Pavilion
New York Worlds Fair, New York, New York, 1964

The Mint • Las Vegas, Nevada, 1961

Citizens National Bank, Oklahoma City, 1968

Lutheran Church • St. Petersberg, Florida, 1967

U.S. Air Force Academy
Colorado Springs, Colorado, 1966

State Capitol Bank • Oklahoma City, Oklahoma, 1964

Kaiser Aluminum Dome • Waikiki, Hawaii, 1959

Glass House Restaurant • Vinita, Oklahoma, 1957

Glass House Restaurant
Vinita, Oklahoma, 1967

The future has arrived. This is utopia. A restaurant with a breathtaking view of the new super-highway below and the countryside that surrounds it is simply out of this world. The Glass House Restaurant—more like a bridge than a house—gracefully spans the Will Rogers Turnpike. Conoco Oil brought us the world's fastest drive-thru in 1957. It was the first restaurant constructed over a United States public highway and a simple solution to cater to motorists passing in both directions. Not only did the Glass House offer gas, gifts and good food, there was a great show too—the constant parade of sparkling cars speeding by below. The ultra-unique eatery is a big hit with tourists and locals. Many local high school proms are held here. As the years pass and America's appetite for fast food increases, the Glass House closes and reopens as the world's largest McDonald's.

1957 Mercury Turnpike Cruiser
Miami Beach Auto Show
Miami Beach, Florida, 1957

Between the name, styling and a long list of optional and standard equipment, the Turnpike Cruiser is one of the most dressed-up and gadget-laden creations ever to roll off of a Detroit assembly line. Mercury's new top-of-the-line model makes its debut spinning on a flying saucer pedestal beneath a space-age light fixture as big as the car. The highly-waxed two-toned orchid-and-white paint scheme and gold anodized aluminum "jet-flo" trim glistens in the light. No other car offers its most unique feature—breezeway ventilation. A pair of five-inch antennae point straight ahead at the top corners of the windshield from air intakes that open and close with a lever. The rear window, the one behind the back seat, goes up and down automatically with the push of a switch. Under the hood is a big 290-horsepower V-8—the most powerful engine Mercury has ever offered. There is no gear shift lever—it has the pushbutton Merc-o-Matic transmission. For safety, the steering wheel is flattened across the top to provide maximum visibility. The instrument cluster and dashboard are padded. Options include seatbelts, power windows, a power seat that "remembers" your favorite position, Climate Master air conditioner-heater and the most convenient option of them all—power lube—but don't forget to push the button every fifty miles! After two model years, 1957 and 1958, the Turnpike Cruiser is discontinued. Should it have been called the Freeway Cruiser?

MERCURY

M

The
TURNPIKE CRUISER

Miami Beach Auto Show
Miami Beach, Florida, 1957

1957 Ford Country Sedan Station Wagon

Saratoga

1957 Chrysler Saratoga

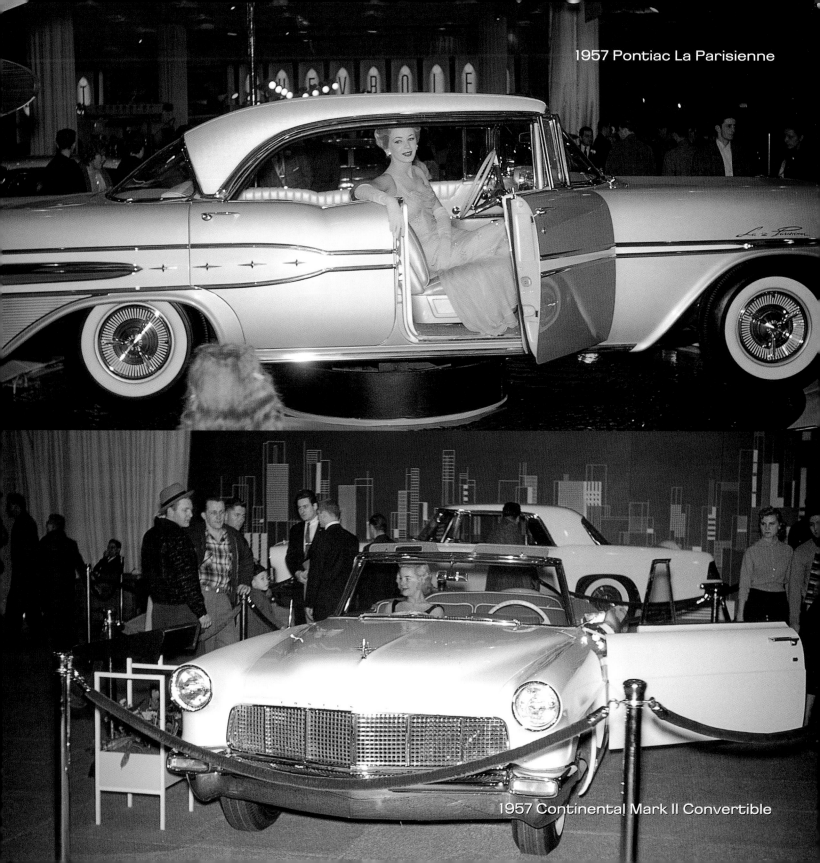

1957 Pontiac La Parisienne

1957 Continental Mark II Convertible

TWA Constellation
Kansas City Municipal Airport
Kansas City, Missouri, 1957

Passengers board the fastest and most luxurious plane in service. With its instantly recognizable triple tails and banana-like fuselage, the Constellation is also the most distinctive. It carries fifty-four passengers and flies at 20,000 feet. Just after Lockheed began manufacturing the Constellation in Burbank, California, in 1944, it became the first commercial airliner able to fly coast-to-coast nonstop. Howard Hughes made the historic flight in a record-setting six hours and fifty-seven minutes. Even fighter planes couldn't match its top speed of 340 miles per hour. In 1945, the Connie, as it affectionately was known, began commercial passenger service with TWA. In 1955, the bigger, faster Super Constella-tion is the first plane to fly nonstop from California to Europe. After 856 Constellations are built, production is discontinued in 1958. TWA begins 707 jet service in March 1959. The last TWA Constellation passenger flight is in 1967. By 2000, just fifty Constellations exist around the world in various states of disrepair. Only three of them are in flying condition. In 2003, the only Constellation able to fly in the United States is repainted in the full TWA color scheme and appears in *The Aviator*, a 2004 movie about the life of Howard Hughes.

TWA Terminal
John F. Kennedy Airport, New York, New York, 1964

A pilot stands waiting for a ride. Five station wagons, including a black 1963 Ford Falcon Squire and white 1964 Dodge crowd the loading and unloading zone. Suitcases sit on the curb. This is a typical airport scene with one exception—the terminal is straight out of a sci-fi fantasy. Unique by any architectural standards, the shape and form of the one-of-a-kind swooping cement sculpture was the final creation of master modern architect Eero Saarinen. Inside, the ticket counters, furnishings, signage, sunken waiting areas, telephone booths and bright orange carpet were all custom-made to complement the organic shape and form. When TWA is absorbed by American Airlines in 2000, the terminal closes. In 2005 JetBlue Airways announces plans to recycle the historic landmark into a flight check-in center.

New York Central Aerotrain
Between New York and Detroit
1956

The train of the future arrives at the station. It is one of two identical prototypes styled and built by General Motors in Detroit. With the oval grille, wrap-around tinted glass and windshield wipers, it looks like a 1956 Oldsmobile morphed into a locomotive. Accompanied by a small army of PR men, the high-fashion trains are touring the country while being auditioned by various railroad companies for future service. The goal is to save the passenger train travel industry by offering ultra-modern styling. Ironically, General Motors manufactures Chevrolets, Pontiacs, Oldsmobiles, Buicks and Cadillacs—so the world's most powerful transportation company is competing with itself. In the summer of 1957, Union Pacific runs an Aerotrain between Los Angeles and Las Vegas. Together the two Aerotrains travel over 600,000 miles on their promotional tour. But the public's response to the futuristic trains is lukewarm at best. By mid-1957 it's clear the space-age trains are no competition to the preferred freedom of traveling on the open road or the rapidly expanding commercial airline industry. Later that year both trains are sold to the Rock Island Railroad for their Chicago commuter service. In 1966 the Aerotrains are retired. One is donated to the National Railroad Museum in Green Bay, Wisconsin, and the other to the National Transportation Museum in Kirkwood, Missouri.

1961 Ford Gyron
Ford Rotunda
Dearborn, Michigan, 1961

A stiff spokesman speaks into a microphone from the passenger chaise longue in the cockpit. He informs visitors of the marvels of the futuristic concept car. Judging by their body language, they are not impressed. Smart potted plants, modern sculpture and a pool with a trickling fountain accessorize the two-tier platform providing an ultramodern atmosphere for the futuristic pop-top car. The Gyron is named for the high-tech device mounted inside that maintains the car's balance on two wheels like a motorcycle. It does the balancing act only when moving forward—just like that favorite toy, the Gyroscope. Little training wheels come down on each side when the car is slowing to a stop, then retract as the car accelerates. There is nothing traditional about this vehicle. Need a steering wheel? Too bad—it doesn't have one. You just lay back and think of the direction that you want to go. And make sure not to slam your finger in the door! Visitors will enjoy this unique display in the Ford Motor Company rotunda until November 9, 1964, when it and everything else inside the historic showcase goes up in flames and burns to the ground. Cause of the fire—a Christmas display that ignites during installation.

Stay Tuned

The talking picture machine is an offspring of the radio. A big picture tube and a speaker cleverly glorified into a fashionable piece of furniture is the ultimate vehicle to promote goods and services. Variety shows, dramas, comedies, game shows, news, sports and serials are actually filler in between commercials sponsored by leading manufacturers and local businesses. The first official television season was 1948. Funnyman Milton Berle becomes the first breakout star on the small screen. On January 1, 1954, the Rose Parade, live from Pasadena, California, is the first coast-to-coast color broadcast. Too bad just twenty-two color televisions sets exist. In 1954 Swanson Frozen Foods introduces the TV dinner—turkey with all the trimmings. It's Thanksgiving every night when you eat your TV dinner on a TV tray in front of the TV. In 1959 NBC debuts *Bonanza*, the first television series in color. President Kennedy tells his fellow Americans to "ask not what your country can do for you; ask what you can do for your country" on a 1960 Sylvania black-and-white Halo Light television framed by a fluorescent light that could be switched on and off with the flip of a switch. On July 20, 1969, TVs around the world tune in to see Neil Armstrong land on the moon. The two-hundred-forty-thousand-mile journey takes four days to complete. He jumps around, collects moon rocks, takes President Nixon's call—the longest long-distance phone call ever—leaves an American flag behind, then gets back on the rocket ship and comes home. That's one small step for a man, one giant leap for mankind.

143

5-4-3-2-1 Blastoff!
Playground Rocket, Location unknown, 1969